For
Susan,
Hubert
&
Andrzej

Today Is Monday Pictures by Eric Carle

PUFFIN BOOKS

Today is Monday
Monday, runner beans

Tuesday, spaghetti
Monday, runner beans

Wednesday, ZOOOOP
Tuesday, spaghetti
Monday, runner beans

Thursday, roast beef
   Wednesday, ZOOOOP
   Tuesday, spaghetti
   Monday, runner beans

Friday, fresh fish
   Thursday, roast beef
   Wednesday, ZOOOOP
   Tuesday, spaghetti
   Monday, runner beans

Saturday, chicken
Friday, fresh fish
Thursday, roast beef
Wednesday, ZOOOOP
Tuesday, spaghetti
Monday, runner beans

Sunday, ice cream
Saturday, chicken
Friday, fresh fish
Thursday, roast beef
Wednesday, ZOOOOP
Tuesday, spaghetti
Monday, runner beans

All you hungry children
Come and eat it up!

Today Is Monday

To - day is Mon - day,____ to - day is Mon - day,

Mon - day runner beans, All you hun - gry chil - dren,

Come and eat it up. To - day is Tues - day,_ to - day is Tues - day,

Tues - day spa - ghet - ti, Mon - day runner beans, All you hun - gry chil - dren

Come and eat it up. To - day is Come and eat it up. ____

Today is Monday, today is Monday
Monday, runner beans
All you hungry children
Come and eat it up.

Today is Tuesday, today is Tuesday
Tuesday, spaghetti
Monday, runner beans
All you hungry children
Come and eat it up.

Today is Wednesday, today is Wednesday
Wednesday, ZOOOOP
Tuesday, spaghetti
Monday, runner beans
All you hungry children
Come and eat it up.

Today is Thursday, today is Thursday
Thursday, roast beef
Wednesday, ZOOOOP
Tuesday, spaghetti
Monday, runner beans
All you hungry children
Come and eat it up.

Today is Friday, today is Friday
Friday, fresh fish
Thursday, roast beef
Wednesday, ZOOOOP
Tuesday, spaghetti
Monday, runner beans
All you hungry children
Come and eat it up.

Today is Saturday, today is Saturday
Saturday, chicken
Friday, fresh fish
Thursday, roast beef
Wednesday, ZOOOOP
Tuesday, spaghetti
Monday, runner beans
All you hungry children
Come and eat it up.

Today is Sunday, today is Sunday
Sunday, ice cream
Saturday, chicken
Friday, fresh fish
Thursday, roast beef
Wednesday, ZOOOOP
Tuesday, spaghetti
Monday, runner beans
All you hungry children
Come and eat it up.

PUFFIN BOOKS

Published by the Penguin Group
Penguin Books Ltd, 27 Wrights Lane, London W8 5TZ, England
Penguin Books USA Inc., 375 Hudson Street, New York, New York 10014, USA
Penguin Books Australia Ltd, Ringwood, Victoria, Australia
Penguin Books Canada Ltd, 10 Alcorn Avenue, Toronto, Ontario, Canada M4V 3B2
Penguin Books (NZ) Ltd, 182–190 Wairau Road, Auckland 10, New Zealand

Penguin Books Ltd, Registered Offices: Harmondsworth, Middlesex, England

First published in the USA by Philomel Books 1993
Published in Great Britain by Hamish Hamilton Ltd 1994
Published in Puffin Books 1996
3 5 7 9 10 8 6 4

Some other Puffin picture books by Eric Carle

THE BAD-TEMPERED LADYBIRD
DO YOU WANT TO BE MY FRIEND
DRAW ME A STAR
THE MIXED-UP CHAMELEON
1, 2, 3 TO THE ZOO
ROOSTER'S OFF TO SEE THE WORLD
THE TINY SEED
THE VERY HUNGRY CATERPILLAR

BROWN BEAR, BROWN BEAR, WHAT DO YOU SEE? *with Bill Martin Jr*
POLAR BEAR, POLAR BEAR, WHAT DO YOU HEAR? *with Bill Martin Jr*